you are enough,
just as you are.

scars are tattoos
with better stories.

life isn't about waiting
for the storm to pass,
but learning to dance
in the rain.

you can't calm the storm,
so stop trying.
calm yourself;
the storm will pass.

the world breaks everyone,
and afterward, some are
strong at the broken places.
- ernest hemingway

some days,
there won't be a song in your
heart.
sing anyway.

every sunset is an
opportunity to
reset.

in our deepest moments
of struggle, we can find
our greatest strength.

your story is
not over yet.

hearts rebuilt from hope
resurrect dreams killed by
hate.
- aberjhani

there is beauty
in vulnerability.

the darkest nights
produce
the brightest stars.

out of suffering
have emerged
the strongest souls.
- kahlil gibran

sorrow looks back,
worry looks around,
but faith looks up.

wounds remind us
where we've been,
they don't dictate
where we're going.

with brave wings,
she flies.

feel everything,
that's the difference
between living and existing.
to feel deeply is a gift;
to hurt deeply,
a testament to our humanity.

emotions are the colours of
the soul.

you,
too,
have survived everything
you've gone through up to
this point.

grief is the price
we pay for
love.
- queen elizabeth ii

there's power in
allowing yourself
to be known and heard.

find solace
in the chaos.

our wounds are often the
openings into the best and
most beautiful part of us. -
david richo

your emotions are valid, not
a sign of weakness.

the wound is the place where
the light enters you. - rumi

hope is the thing with
feathers that perches in the
soul. - emily dickinson

feelings are just visitors,
let them come and go.

when one door of happiness
closes, another opens. -
helen keller t

here's a crack in everything,
that's how the light gets in.
- leonard cohen

the heart that aches is a
heart that beats.

breathe.

you're going to be okay.

pain demands to be felt.

there is a sacredness in
tears. - washington irving

dare to feel, for only
through feelings do we truly
touch the heart of life.

loss carves us into kinder,
more empathetic souls.

you are not broken, you are
breaking through.

even the darkest clouds can't
obscure the light forever.

where there is love, there is
life. - mahatma Gandhi

we bleed, we heal, we rise.

it's okay to crumble, that's
how ruins become art.

silence isn't empty, it's
full of answers.

tears are words the heart
can't say.

to be human is to be
beautifully flawed.

life's roughest storms prove
the strength of our anchors.

hurt is the price for an open
heart.

suffering is not holding you;
you are holding suffering. -
buddha

embrace uncertainty.

some of the most beautiful
chapters in our lives won't
have a title until much
later.

don't let the past hold you,
but let it guide you.

in the depth of winter, i
finally learned that within
me there lay an invincible
summer. - albert camus

broken crayons still color.

breathe. it's just a bad day,
not a bad life.

vulnerability is the
birthplace of innovation,
creativity, and change. -
brené brown

the best way out is always
through. - robert frost

even shattered glass can
reflect the light.

love is the bridge between
you and everything. - rumi

tears are the river of life;
let them flow.

every pain makes you more
human, every tear more
reflective.

life doesn't get easier, we
just become stronger.

stars can't shine without
darkness.

sometimes, we need to break
to find out how strong we
really are.

the soul would have no
rainbow if the eyes had no
tears.

the heaviest rain often comes
out of the darkest clouds. -
rumi

life is tough, but so are
you.

the most beautiful hearts
have known suffering and
found their way out of the
depths.

when everything seems to be
going against you, remember
that the aeroplane takes off
against the wind, not with
it. - henry ford

we grow through what we go
through.

embrace the glorious mess
that you are. - elizabeth
gilbert

when it rains, look for
rainbows.

when it's dark, look for
stars.

bravery isn't the absence of
fear but the action despite
its presence.

the rose's rarest essence
lives in the thorns. - rumi

sometimes, the worst pain
brings about the best change.

your heart knows the way; run
in that direction. - rumi

without rain, nothing grows.
embrace the storms in your
life.

emotions aren't weaknesses;
they're reminders we're
alive.

love more, worry less.

be a warrior, not a worrier.

the sun will rise and we will
try again. turn your face to
the sun and the shadows fall
behind you. - maori proverb

when you come out of the
storm, you won't be the same
person who walked in. -
haruki murakami

the only way to move forward
is to face the wind.

drenched in rain, yet rising
to touch the sun. let your
tears water the seeds of your
future happiness. - steve
maraboli

emotion is the poetry of
life.

you were never created to
live depressed, defeated,
guilty, ashamed, or unworthy.
you were created to be
victorious.

wear your scars as your best
attire. a stunning dress made
of hellfire. - daniel saint

the most beautiful people we
have known are those who have
known defeat, known
suffering, known struggle,
known loss, and have found
their way out of those
depths. - elisabeth kübler-
ross

to weep is to make less the
depth of grief. - william
shakespeare

fall down seven times, stand
up eight. - japanese proverb

in tears, there's a healing.
in vulnerability, strength.

our greatest glory is not in
never falling, but in rising
every time we fall. -
confucius

out of difficulties grow
miracles. - jean de la
bruyère

no storm can last forever. it
will never rain 365 days
consecutively.

keep in mind that trouble
comes to pass, not to stay.

no storm, not even the one in
your life, can last forever.
- iyanla vanzant

with every tear comes the
promise of a rainbow.

the lotus blooms most
beautifully from the deepest
and thickest mud. - buddhist
proverb

every tear shed carves a
river path of strength
through the mountains of our
struggles.

tears are liquid love.
emotion flowing, showing just
how deeply we feel.

the greater the storm, the
brighter the rainbow.

with pain comes strength.

shadows cannot exist without
light.

beauty begins the moment you
decide to be yourself. - coco
chanel

the world gives you so much
pain, and here you are making
gold out of it. - rupi kaur

you have to feel. you have to
risk. sometimes it's worth
it.

where words fail, emotions
speak.

there's strength in every
tear, hope in every smile.

the heart knows a hundred
thousand ways to speak. -
rumi

when pain knocks on your
door, let strength answer.

emotion is the language of
the soul. listen closely.

i am made of tears and
resilience.

to heal a wound, you need to
stop touching it.

what feels like the end is
often the beginning.

your pain is the breaking of
the shell that encloses your
understanding. - kahlil
Gibran

every emotion is a
brushstroke in the painting
of our lives.

i am bent, but not broken.

in the depth of emotion lies
the richness of life.

with new tears comes new
growth.

your pain is a school into
which you were meant to
learn. - aeschylus

emotions are the melodies of
our soul.

every time we endure, we
build the chapters of our
story.

the world needs more of what
you've been hiding.

in pain and laughter, life
dances its eternal dance.

the heart was made to be
broken. - oscar wilde

resilience is not about
having a backbone. it's about
strengthening the muscles
around our backbone. - sheryl
Sandberg

our deepest emotions are our
most authentic self.

in our wounds, we find our
truest selves.

healing is an art. it takes
time, it takes practice. it
takes love.

the most powerful words are
often drenched in emotion.

tears are the silent language
of grief. - voltaire

you are more resilient than
you believe, more loved than
you know.

let your emotions flow like a
river, clearing out the
debris of the past.

it's okay to feel, to heal,
to be real.

emotions are the messengers
of the soul.

pain nourishes courage.

you can't be brave if you've
only had wonderful things
happen to you. - mary tyler
moore

every tear tells a tale,
every smile shares a secret.

growth and comfort do not
coexist. - ginni rometty

love is the emotion that a
woman feels always for a
poodle dog and sometimes for
a man. - george jean nathan

life breaks us all, and
afterward, many are strong at
the broken places. - ernest
hemingway

emotion is energy in motion.

the human soul is a sea,
bounded by tears and smiles.

to hide feelings when you are
near crying is the secret of
dignity. - dejan stojanovic

life is full of beauty.
notice it. notice the
bumblebee, the small child,
and the smiling faces. smell
the rain, and feel the wind.
- ashley smith

emotions aren't a sign of
weakness but a symbol of
being alive.

every challenge, every
adversity, contains within it
the seeds of opportunity and
growth. - roy t. bennett

feelings are much like waves.
we can't stop them from
coming, but we can choose
which ones to surf.

where there is emotion, there
is the essence of life.

be the love you never
received. - rune lazuli

sometimes, letting go is an
act of far greater power than
defending or holding on.

let your tears come. let them
water your soul. - eileen
mayhew

the deeper the feelings, the
harder they are to express.

embrace uncertainty.

some of the most beautiful
chapters in our lives won't
have a title until much
later. - bob goff

emotions are the spices of
life, giving it flavour and
richness.

healing is a matter of time,
but it is sometimes also a
matter of opportunity. -
hippocrates

every emotion, if it's
sincere, is involuntary. -
mark twain

our greatest battles are with
our own minds. - jameson
frank

emotions move us, drive us,
and tell the tales of our
lives.

emotions are the truest
poets.

in every tear, there's a
lesson. in every smile, a
blessing.

Pain is inevitable, but
suffering is optional. -
haruki murakami

the walls we build around us
to keep sadness out also keep
out the joy. - jim rohn

life is not about how fast
you run or how high you
climb, but how well you
bounce.

don't let pain define you,
let it refine you.

the strongest people aren't
always the people who win,
but the people who don't give
up when they lose.

emotion is more powerful than
reason. emotion is the
driving force behind thinking
and reasoning. - robert
greene

your emotions are the slaves
to your thoughts, and you are
the slave to your emotions. -
elizabeth gilbert

vulnerability is the
birthplace of love,
belonging, joy, courage,
empathy, and creativity. -
brené brown

sometimes we're tested. not
to show our weaknesses, but
to discover our strengths.

emotion is the bridge to
action, the path to memory,
and the key to connection.

in silence, the heart learns
a song.

sometimes, emotions are the
only proof that something
real exists inside us.

we can endure much more than
we think we can; all human
experience testifies to that.
- yasmin mogahed

hearts can heal. broken
dreams can mend. always
remember, every end is a new
beginning.

emotions are the compass of
the soul.

life is not a series of
agonizing throws. it's a
mosaic of delightful ones. -
sanober khan

emotions are like passing
storms; let them come and let
them go.

the emotion that can break
your heart is sometimes the
very one that heals it. -
nicholas sparks

trust the timing of your
life. what's meant to be will
always find a way.

tears are the silent language
of the soul.

sometimes the strongest among
us are the ones who smile
through silent pain, cry
behind closed doors, and
fight battles nobody knows
about.

stay true to your feelings,
for they are the gateways to
your soul.

to love and be loved is to
feel the sun from both sides.
- david viscott

the heart feels what the eyes
cannot see. the most
beautiful things in the world
cannot be seen or touched,
they are felt with the heart.
- antoine de saint-exupéry

you have within you right
now, everything you need to
deal with whatever the world
can throw at you. - brian
tracy

it's okay to be a glowstick;
sometimes we need to break
before we shine.

your feelings are valid. they
are the echo of your soul's
song.

behind every tear is a story.
behind every smile is a
journey. emotion is the
universal language, the
bridge between disparate
worlds.

every emotion felt is a step
towards understanding oneself
better.

tears are how our heart
speaks when our lips cannot
describe how much we've been
hurt.

life is made of moments;
emotions make them
unforgettable.

sometimes, emotions are the puzzles, and time is the key.

keep feeling, keep fighting,
keep living.

your story isn't calm. the
road has been chaotic at
times, filled with detours
and rain and loss so sudden,
and soon.

sometimes the bliss was so
elevated your heart could
hardly hold it.

and you've always loved to
tell a good story. - victoria
erickson

the soul's music plays
through the symphony of
emotions.

your feelings are your
superpower.

let emotions be your guide,
not your anchor.